This Book
Belongs to
Connie Duarte Soares

Santa Clara
Ca.

Given By

Evangelina Mancibo

Recipes
from the
Portuguese
of
Provincetown

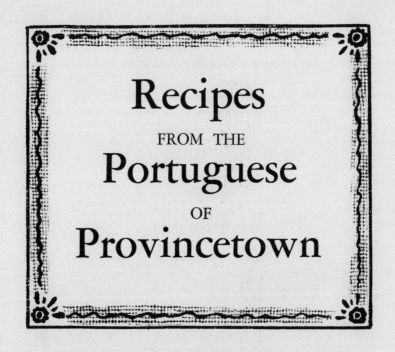

Recipes

FROM THE

Portuguese

OF

Provincetown

By

MARGARET H. KOEHLER

Illustrated by

RUDOLF CZUFIN

Foreword by

SENHORA DONA MARIA LUIZA PATRICIO

The Chatham Press, Inc. Riverside, Connecticut

Library of Congress Catalog Card Number: 72-93260
SBN 85699-061-2 (cloth)
SBN 85699-060-4 (paper)

DESIGNED BY CHRISTOPHER HARRIS

Printed in the United States of America.

Contents

*Querido Deus que o outro ano em éste dia estaremos todos
juntos com vida e saúde para celebrarmos esta festa
com paz e alegria.*

Dear God, may we in another year on this day again be
gathered together with life and health so that we may
celebrate this holiday with peace and happiness.

OLD PORTUGUESE NEW YEAR'S PRAYER
Courtesy of Eugenio Teixeira

ACKNOWLEDGEMENTS

I would like to express special thanks to my husband, Chuck, who has gone on countless treks and happily relished untold quantities of Portuguese food in the interest of gathering this material; to Madeline Thompson, who is getting to be an expert researcher, is a great companion on all sorts of safaris and interviews, and who always manages to have "the facts" right at her fingertips; to Rudy Arruda for sharing some of his heirloom recipes and the story of how his family made linguiça; to Joel O'Brien, whose mother, Mary Heaton Vorse, wrote a wonderful book about Provincetown and who has shared both his friends and facts with me; to Rose and Joe Silva and many other Portuguese-American friends and acquaintances for telling me about the dances, customs and festivals of older days; and to Al and Kathy Giddings for lending their culinary expertise to an evaluation of the recipes.

Foreword

Few subjects will find such all-round popularity in this controversial age as the culinary art — in which Portugal excels. If it is true that the surest way to a man's heart is through what he eats, Portuguese food has won Portugal many friends abroad.

The Portuguese way of life contains a distillation of contacts between the most diverse peoples of the earth, and nowhere else is this better reflected than in Portuguese cookery. The explorer returning home always brought something new from far-off lands to mingle with his native fare and give it its distinctive flavor.

That so many recipes could be compiled from a single Portuguese community in the United States provides eloquent testimony to the manner in which the Portuguese like to live away from Portugal, freely mixing with other peoples, taking something from new found tradition to enrich their own, and above all, sharing with others their joys, their laughter, their music and their wine.

—SENHORA DONA MARIA LUIZA PATRICIO,
Wife of the Portuguese Ambassador
to the United Nations

Preface

There is an intricate link between people and their food: a sort of invisible chain that spans oceans and unites continents. Think of Yorkshire pudding, for example, and instantly England comes to mind. By the same token, spaghetti evokes Italy, knockwurst could belong nowhere else but to Germany, les escargots are purely French and goulash completely Hungarian.

Many times immigrants could bring along little else on their difficult journey to a new land except memories of their homeland, its traditions, customs and special foods. These dishes, which frequently had national, ethnic or religious symbolism, were recreated in the new homes with adaptations to suit the available ingredients — but they still smelled and tasted much the same. The recipes, in turn, became heirlooms of a kind, evoking nostalgia and being passed on for generations to come.

The association between food and national origin that we see today is particularly strong for Americans whose families immigrated within the past fifty to one hundred years. For example, Rudolf Czufin, the illustrator of this book, vividly remembers the Hungarian dishes his mother made when he was a child. She later passed her recipes on to his non-Hungarian wife and they are still very much a part of the family menu.

Of all the cuisines in this country — and there are as many as there are nationalities represented in the American spectrum — the Portuguese is one of the most interesting but least well known. The Portuguese have always been a seafaring people, and so they make delicious meals featuring fish in all its varieties. The use of spice as a preservative goes far back into history, and thus many of their meats even today, particularly the linguiça sausage used in so many ways, are well spiced. They also favored sweet wines on festive occasions, and so made many kinds of little cakes and fritters to go with them — and still do.

There are Portuguese-Americans living in many parts of the United States, but the largest concentrations can be found on the east and west coasts, especially in the fishing and seaport centers there. Of these many towns, Provincetown, Massachusetts, has been chosen as the focal point of this book because it is, literally, a Portuguese-flavored community. The majority of its permanent residents owe some, if not all, of their heritage to Portugal. It has been estimated that eighty-five percent of the year-round Provincetown population is at least partly of Portuguese ancestry.

To understand the reasons for the very special characteristics of any national cuisine, it is first necessary to know something about the history and the customs of the people. In delving into both about the Portuguese-Americans, I quickly realized that the avenue to knowledge branched into a number of roads which radiated outwards. Although most of the Portuguese of Provincetown trace their ancestry to the Azores, other Portuguese-American lineage goes back to the mainland of Portugal itself or to the Cape Verde Islands, Madeira, or one of the other outlying colonies.

Finally, in singling out Provincetown as the locale for this book, no offense is intended toward the many other Portuguese-American communities. They, too, have interesting histories and talented chefs who may have not only appetizing variations of the recipes included here but entirely new ones which might be added. Comments — whether good or bad — are invited so that they may be included in future editions.

—MARGARET H. KOEHLER
Orleans, Massachusetts

Portuguese Provincetown

There are really two Provincetowns which, like summer and winter residents of the same house, share that tip of land which all but tumbles into the sea at the end of Cape Cod. The scenery, except for seasonal differences, remains the same while everything else changes.

Most people know the Provincetown of "the season" when, for ten or twelve weeks of summer, it seems as if all the world crowds together in a kaleidoscope of color, excitement and gaiety. People watchers fill the benches outside the old Town Hall or sip espresso under the awnings of sidewalk cafés while an endless procession of young and old pass by, drawn to the variety of gift shops, craft displays, restaurants and other entertainment. At night the town is alive with summer theater, and bright lights and modern music reflect and reverberate over the stillness of the harbor and the Province Lands dunes.

But summer *does* end in P'town; not right at Labor Day as it once did, but more gradually now as fall's patina takes over. One day, quite surprisingly, Provincetown resumes its role as a Portuguese fishing village with such a distinct personality that, having experienced both, one cannot help wonder which is "real."

Yet, if you know Provincetown, even as you ask the question the answer becomes obvious. Portuguese Provincetown is the real thing, and it has been so for over a century. With the end of the tourist season, the dark-haired, dark-eyed, olive-skinned Portuguese-Americans reclaim their streets and resume their own way of life. Then, if you walk along a narrow street, you may catch a whiff of something yeasty and wonderful, and find yourself passing a bakery window laden with round loaves of fragrant, fresh bread: Portuguese bread.

A bit later, going by a restaurant, you may see a sign in the window that says: "Portuguese soup today." If you are curious you investigate and at once open up a whole gastronomic world which, in turn, will pique your interest in the people who have made such delightful dishes: the Portuguese, who have brought, not only to Cape

Cod but to anywhere they have settled, a culture and cuisine which most of us know very little about.

Long before Columbus, the Pilgrims and other celebrated adventurers reached the New World, Portuguese sailors braved the sea in small ships, undaunted by the perils they often encountered. In 1418 they discovered the island of Madeira and in 1427 reached the Azores. By 1460 they had explored and colonized the Cape Verde Islands off the coast of Africa, and had even sailed as far as the western shores of India and circumnavigated the African continent. They were called "sons of the sea" and were acknowledged as the world's greatest navigators. A Jesuit missionary named Antonio Vieira summed up their courage and curiosity when he said, "God gave the Portuguese a small country for a cradle, but the whole world for a grave."

The first recorded voyage of the Portuguese to the North Atlantic was that of Gaspar Corte Real, a nobleman from the Azores who embarked on a great search for the elusive western route to Asia. Believing that the coveted passage lay to the north, he reached the North American coast in 1500, landing first at Newfoundland and then venturing as far south as the Hudson Strait before going home to Portugal. The next year he returned with three ships and, probably at Cabot's Cape Breton, saw Indians wearing Venetian earrings which led him to believe he had at last found Asia. Sending two of his ships home, the brave man continued his exploration northward and was never heard from again.

A few years later Gaspar's brother, Miguel Corte Real, was sent out by King Emanuel to learn the fate of Gaspar's expedition. Miguel also failed to return to Portugal, but many historians insist that he "definitely and undeniably" left an inscription on the Dighton Rock in Taunton, Massachusetts, which has been dated about 1511. The rock has now been enshrined in a state park of the same name, and advocates of the theory claim that the Corte Real inscription proves that the first European to actually set foot on the continental United States was Portuguese.

Ships' records from later centuries continue to tell the story. For example, of twenty-two Portuguese galleons which left Lisbon between 1590 and 1593, only two returned safely to port. Of thirty-three that went out between 1606 and 1608, only seven returned. Yet despite such losses, the Portuguese continued to maintain their sovereignty of the seas in the seventeenth century, opening up trade routes throughout the world.

While these adventurers pushed further and further outwards, many others left Portugal with their families to settle in the Azores, the Cape Verde Islands and other islands and colonies as far away as Burma and China. Since Portugal itself was a poor country, her people literally had to go beyond her borders to make a living as the population increased. Second only to their abilities as seamen was their knowledge of farming. They cultivated the soil, growing pineapples and oranges and tea on the gracefully terraced hillsides of their islands. They had a way with the earth, especially when it came to raising fruits and vegetables, and this skill has never been lost.

The Portuguese began coming to the United States in numbers during the first half of the nineteenth century, when both whaling and fishing were rapidly growing seacoast industries. Whaling ships put in at Portuguese islands, especially the Cape Verdes, to replenish their supplies and give the crews shore leave. After months at sea, the men set about celebrating with such vehemence that they were usually far from ready to go back aboard when sailing time came. Often those who had been "crimped" — drugged or simply knocked out and taken aboard ship against their will — deserted the ships entirely. The captains, in turn, were forced to seek new crews and by one means or another impressed local Portuguese men into service. When they reached the United States, they jumped ship and sought work in the new land, usually in or around the seaports where they landed. Thus today not only Provincetown but New Bedford, Fall River, Falmouth, Harwich, Lowell and Gloucester, Massachusetts, all have large Portuguese populations, as do many other New England towns. New Bedford, where many settled then and later, has been called the "Capital of the Portuguese in the United States."

In later years other young Portuguese men came to America to escape conscription into the King's military service; some were so desperate as to sail across the Atlantic in small boats. There is no record of those who failed to reach our shores, but their numbers may have been considerable. Still more arrived with their families through Ellis Island in New York Harbor to move on to already established Portuguese communities in coastal New England.

The Portuguese who came from the Cape Verde Islands were known as *Bravas*. Their blood is actually a mixture of Arabic, Portuguese and Sudanese African. Many of their descendants still live on the Cape and comprise a large portion of the Portuguese population in Harwich and Falmouth. For the most part they have now given up the sea in favor of farming, or have undertaken business or professional pursuits.

Over the years the *Bravas* have largely been responsible for the success of the cranberry industry, working as pickers in the vast bogs of the Upper Cape and the Wareham area. Others chose Fal-

mouth and helped it become one of the great strawberry growing centers of America. They literally wrested the fields and bogs from waste areas of scrub pine, oak and sand.

Until the mid-nineteenth century, Provincetown's population was of almost solidly Yankee stock. But even in its very early years of settlement during the late 1600's, it had been viewed by the more stalwart Bostonians in somewhat the same light as summertime P'town is today — as a maverick which they wished would simply go away. In the words of historian Henry Kittredge, it was a place where "miscellaneous smugglers, 'Portege' whalemen, French privateers and colonial fishermen who camped there for the summer, all plied their trades with as much freedom as if Provincetown had been a remote island of the Spanish Main." The "riotous doings" so shocked the ears of the Boston magistrates that in 1714 the town was placed under the rule of the more righteous town of Truro and all visiting fishermen charged four shillings a week during their Provincetown sojourns. By 1727, however, the town had learned its lesson and was granted its own charter.

Still, piety did not bring prosperity. In 1755 ten houses sheltered the town's entire population and in 1764 the census-taker ignored the place completely. Fishing, however, was a rapidly growing business and Provincetown offered a superb harbor that gave access to some of the finest grounds right offshore as well as the Grand Banks of Newfoundland and the Labrador Coast. By 1790 the Provincetown fleet numbered twenty vessels and by 1802 had grown to thirty-three, with a catch valued at over $100,000 worth of cod alone, to say nothing of the mackerel, herring, flounder, halibut and other fish.

Fishing continued to expand as the main business of the Provincetonians until, by the 1850's, the town was in close competition with Gloucester as the principal fishing port of the northeast coast. The Provincetown fleet at its prime exceeded one hundred vessels, and must have been a magnificent sight to behold when a large portion was at anchor in the harbor! Along with this growth came the need for kindred industries alongshore. Some ten salt works were producing eight thousand hogsheads of salt a year; five buildings were used for smoking herring and ninety for storing fish.

While all this activity produced a thriving industry, the local population could not keep pace with the demand for labor, because many Yankee boys found better opportunities off-Cape or ashore, preferring not to risk their lives and comforts on the fishing smacks. Thus the captains and owners sought crews elsewhere, and found them in the excellent Portuguese seamen.

The first Portuguese to settle in Provincetown is said to have been Emanuel Caton, who arrived in 1822. According to Nancy Smith who wrote *The Provincetown Book,* Emanuel ran away from his home in Lisbon as a boy and sailed on a ship that was captured by pirates. While the rest of the crew was made to walk the plank, he was kept aboard as a slave to the captain. When the ship put in at Provincetown with its captain sick and near death, Emanuel was allowed to leave. He married a local girl and lived to an old age, a respected citizen of the town.

Whether Emanuel was first or not, the Portuguese came in ever increasing numbers to the port to settle and work at fishing, whaling and the many related occupations ashore. When the seas ran high and storms came up, it was said that the Portuguese crews were the last into harbor and usually brought the largest catches. It was they, too, who sailed the trim, seaworthy schooners designed for use on the Georges Banks, those treacherous shoals that lie some eighty miles off Chatham. A story is still told of the fishing record made by the Portuguese skipper of the *Julie Costa* who sailed from Provincetown Harbor to the grounds off Highland Light, caught 150,000 pounds of cod and took his catch to Boston — all in the seventeen hours between 6 A.M. and 11 P.M.!

By 1896, there were some two thousand Portuguese residents in Provincetown and the fishing industry, as well as the town itself, was firmly in their hands. Agnes Edwards, writing about Provincetown in 1918 in *Cape Cod, Old and New,* described the town as:

Portuguese — Portuguese — Portuguese everywhere. They are the fishermen, the storekeepers; the men work; the children skip rope on the sidewalk; their daughters are waitresses in the hotels and teachers in the school. . . . There are Portuguese women who cannot speak English; Portuguese men who marry the daughters of Cape Cod stock. There is every shade of color from almost black to a creamy olive, and every grade of refinement in their foreign countenances. Some come from the Azores, and some from Portugal, and there is more or less a feud between them, and more or less resentment against them all by the natives. But they are a thrifty, law-abiding people, and here, as elsewhere on the Cape, their industry and picturesqueness contribute something not without value to the general life.

Mrs. Edwards had been a long-time vacationer on Cape Cod and wrote somewhat nostalgically of her journeys in earlier years and the many changes she had seen. She mentioned that, since the automobile had come into prominent use in the previous decade, Provincetown had also come into a new era. There were now tourists who drove down for "an alluring weekend trip," and summer colonists who were "artistic and literary folk." But "the most radical change of all," she wrote, "has been the gradual establishment of the Portuguese in the first home of our forefathers. Coming, as those original settlers came, across the ocean from the east, these smiling men and women have, without any spectacular ovation, silently, persistently, inconspicuously achieved the occupation of Provincetown."

This was true in 1918, and still is. Today, the Portuguese of Provincetown are "Cape Codders" just as much as are their Yankee neighbors, and numerically they have the upper hand. If you glance down the Provincetown tax list you will find that there are more Portuguese surnames than any other national origin. And even the supposedly Anglo-Saxon names can be deceptive. "Perry," for instance, was once "Pereira," "Deers" came from "Dias," and so on.

Outwardly, the residential areas of Provincetown are old New England Colonial, with a charm that makes some people remember English fishing villages. There are prim white cottages and staid, dark-shuttered Captains' houses that in some places all but jostle each other for space. But, as you walk along winding streets and through narrow lanes, you will also find ornate statues of holy figures encased in glass, some of them beautifully painted with blue robes and gilded so that crowns and halos sparkle gold in the sun. Set in front of a typically Cape Cod house, the combination symbolizes this blend of Yankee and Portuguese.

I have a friend in Provincetown who expresses this particular sense of pride as well as anyone. Her father sailed across the Atlantic from the Azores in a fishing boat about the time of the American Civil War. "They came from Portugal in those days to escape the draft," she says, "and by the time they got here all they had left to eat was molasses." Now Rose Silva and her husband Joe, both in their seventies, live in a house that sits atop a hill overlooking Provincetown Harbor. Pine trees brush their picture window, framing a view of pure beauty that seems to stretch all the way to Portugal.

Cape Cod is, in fact, about as close to Portugal as one can get and still be on the American mainland. If you stand on the outer beach looking east across the water and project in your imagination a ship sailing toward the rising sun, you would, via the invisible 42nd meridian, finally come to land directly on the coast of Portugal.

Like most people who have come here from other places, the Portuguese-Americans belong first to the United States and, although they have been discriminated against, "resented" as Mrs. Edwards put it, they have retained the spiritual and practical links with the traditions of their homeland. There are few Portuguese housewives today who do not know how to make at least some of the favorite dishes from recipes brought by their ancestors and passed down from mother to daughter. Even a Cape girl whose only claim to Portuguese ancestry may be a single grandparent is familiar with this fine cuisine.

In 1540, the Portuguese historian João de Barros, in describing Portuguese accomplishments throughout the world, said, "The coats of arms and the monumental pillars which the Portuguese have set up are material things, and time can destroy them; but time cannot destroy the way of life and the language which the Portuguese have left behind them in those lands." It is hard to imagine what Provincetown would be like were the Portuguese to leave it: surely a deserted village, at least off-season. But the loss would be greater than that. For the Portuguese have made a contribution to Provincetown that can be summed up, as one anonymous writer did, by saying, "The southern rose has been grafted to the sturdy oak of New England neatness and thrift."

Festivals and
Feast Days

If there is one thing the Portuguese have contributed to their neat and thrifty Yankee neighbors, it is the gaiety of their festivals, dances and pageantry. Food, of course, is an important part of these occasions and many of the recipes in this book have symbolic meanings attached to them.

Most of the festive occasions such as Christmas, Easter, the Blessing of the Fleet or the celebration of the "name" day of a favorite saint are connected with religion. I once asked a friend to tell me when Saint John's Day was. She went home, did a bit of research and called me up. "Which Saint John do you want?" she asked. "There are twenty-seven of them!"

Music and dancing, processions and parades, religious blessings and sacraments; all are part of the cultural heritage that has been passed from generation to generation. Today these celebrations are not on the same scale as they were in former years, but they still are very much a part of the local scene. The Portuguese, perhaps more so than other nationalities, have tried to retain at least the major traditional feast days and festivals even though the young people tend to dismiss them as being "old-fashioned."

One organization which is contributing toward the preservation of these customs is the Portuguese-American Civic League. Membership in the league derives from all the New England communities with sizeable Portuguese populations. Conventions are held at regular intervals; meetings are three-day gala affairs that take place in one or another of the sponsoring communities, often the home town of the presiding chairman. In addition to the business sessions, there are banquets and balls with the traditional foods, music and dances. The final day of the convention, Sunday, is always highlighted by the celebration of Mass with the sermon spoken in Portuguese.

The Provincetown Art Association has also collaborated with this effort in recent years and now sponsors an annual Portuguese Night. It is usually held in midsummer and includes Portuguese music and dancing, exhibits and refreshments.

The person largely responsible for making this possible is Mrs. Grace Collinson, herself of Portuguese descent and the director of the town's Senior Citizens' Center. She has also taken a giant step toward the re-establishment of tradition by arranging for the display of the time-honored *Menino Jesus* at the Senior Citizens' Center during Christmas Week.

In a not very distant past, the *Menino Jesus* was the core of the

Christmas celebration in Portuguese homes, and it could be as elaborate or simple as a family wished to make it. Today the only one in Provincetown that many people see is set up in the Senior Citizens' Center.

Menino Jesus means "Little Boy Jesus," and the figure often used is that of the standing Christ Child, rather than of the Holy Infant. The effect of the entire scene is triangular. It consists of a series of shelves, usually covered with white cloth, arranged so that the center top is the focal point of the display. Here are placed the holy figures, with the Christ Child at the forefront. Traditionally, the figures themselves were true works of art, brought from the "Old Country" and having special significance to the owners. Not only the Holy Family but many of the favorite saints are also included, the total number depending on how elaborate the display is to be.

On the remaining shelves there may be a variety of things, but there are always wheat and candles. Wheat is sprouted in dishes and placed around the display to represent the Resurrection, and sheaves of wheat added to represent the staff of life. White candles glowing throughout represent the Light.

From this point on the *Menino Jesus* becomes an individual thing, and can vary considerably, although the effect remains the same. For the Senior Citizens' *Menino Jesus,* the members bring their own figures. The center of the display is encased in an ornately decorated glass oratorio and the effect is outstanding.

Roses are strewn throughout the shelves since the rose, as Mrs. Collinson explained, "is the flower of Portugal. Roses bloom in Portugal at Christmas and are plentiful. The Portuguese are a practical people: they have always used what they have." There is also a "curative crown" which is believed to have rare healing powers. And there are beautifully carved gray doves representing the Holy Spirit, some of which have bright red ribbons tied to them to give thanks for wishes that have been granted.

At the base of the triangle, a number of shoes are placed, filled with coal, oranges and nuts. Traditionally the oranges represent happiness, the coal humility, and the nuts fertility.

Throughout the week-long observance of Christmas, people drop in to sit quietly by the *Menino Jesus* or chat with one another. Many of them are older people and their thoughts must often turn to the days when every home had its own *Menino Jesus.*

Sometimes, if a family's display were relatively small, it was set in the front window or, if it was placed elsewhere, the window was filled with lighted candles. Either was an invitation to friends and strangers alike to drop in and share a continual "open house" from Christmas Eve to New Year's Day. When guests came, they were served homemade beach plum or elderberry wine, or the Portuguese port or madeira, and special holiday sweets such as *trutas* and *suspiros.* "In the old days," Rose Silva recalls, "anyone was welcome. In fact, strangers were the most welcome and honored guests of all."

Music, too, was very much a part of the celebration. On Christmas Eve men would gather in groups to go from house to house singing carols in their soft, swishing, native tongue and strumming their seven-stringed *guitarres.* Before the days of strict immigration and customs laws, Portuguese ships often anchored in Provincetown Harbor and their bands would come ashore to stroll through the streets, serenading the townspeople.

Today the Silvas and most other Portuguese put out their creches, but no longer take the time and care to arrange the triangle. "Open house" is usually confined to family and friends, and the traditional serenading is limited to an occasional neighborhood carol sing. "Gradually the old traditions have died out," one old man told me. "The passage of time, deaths in the family, lack of interest on the part of the young — all these take their toll."

Yet Provincetown is far from bleak at Christmas! Local efforts are being made to restore the Christmas serenading and once again fill the streets with beautiful music. Around the Town Hall parking meters are removed and gaily decorated Christmas trees inserted into the empty holes, setting the mood for a Christmas that is still quite different from any place else.

Easter, as might be expected, is nearly as important to the Portuguese as Christmas. There are traditional dishes such as the *Massa Sovada,* a special kind of sweet bread with whole, uncooked eggs pressed into the tops of the loaves before they are baked. Children often get the eggs, and a friend of mine remembers his mother dotting the bread with enough raw eggs so that each child would have one. Easter is a day primarily for church-going, for family dinners and for visiting.

Of all the religious festivals, however, the most well-known is the Blessing of the Fleet, traditionally held each year on the last Sunday of June, at the height of the tourist season. Thousands of onlookers come to Provincetown, or to New Bedford or Gloucester

where similar blessings are held, to witness this event. Gloucester, in fact, offers two fleet blessings — one in Portuguese and one in Italian. The town can use them both: probably no other community has lost so many men to the sea.

At Provincetown, a morning service is conducted in the Church of Saint Peter, the Fisherman. Then members of the fishing fleet carry the statue of Saint Peter in a procession through the town to MacMillan Wharf. Usually a Bishop is in attendance and, at the head of the wharf, he and his entourage hold a kind of court. Colorfully bedecked fishing boats sail past the pier and are blessed, one by one, with thanks for the success of past years and an invocation for a prosperous new fishing season. Perhaps no better words can express the symbolic importance of this festive, yet deeply religious, occasion than the old Portuguese motto:

Our Saviour fed the Multitude
Two thousand years ago.
We are Fishermen.

Other special dates during the summer include June 13th, Saint Anthony's Day, which is a favorite day for weddings. In Portugal this day is so highly regarded that nuptial Masses are held en masse throughout the land. The Feast of São Joao (not to be confused with the major Feast of Saint John on December 27th) is remembered by older Portuguese as a summertime feast day when men made large wooden crosses and decorated them with greens. To these they would attach fresh fruit and loaves of Portuguese bread wrapped in cellophane and auction the food off to raise money for the church. The bread, especially, brought high prices from the tourists.

On the first weekend in August the Feast of the Blessed Sacrament is held in New Bedford at Madeira Field. It is said to be the largest Portuguese festival in the world, drawing crowds of Portuguese-Americans from all over the east, as well as many non-Portuguese who come to join the fun. The celebration honors a pledge made in 1914 by four men from Madeira who reached the shores of America after a particularly harrowing voyage across the Atlantic and vowed to remember forever the Providence which spared them.

In Provincetown and elsewhere during the summer tourist season, various other Portuguese fairs and arts and crafts displays are held. Not only are the Portuguese good cooks but their cleverness extends to the creation of delicate needlework and embroidery and beautiful knitted or crocheted garments and other objects that blend the bright colors they love so much in new and interesting ways. Rose Silva spends her winter hours crocheting intricate squares which she sews together into snug lap robes, each made in a different color pattern. These she bestows upon her friends who treasure them both for their practical comfort and as family heirlooms.

Rose likes to talk about the old days as she crochets and remembers with nostalgia the Portuguese dances at the Provincetown Town

Hall every Saturday night. "The girls would all wear bright-colored costumes," she remembers. "First there would be a procession with the girls in one line and the men in another. And then we would have the dance."

The favorite Portuguese dance is called *La Charmarita,* a name derived from the verb *charmar* which means "to allure," and it is easy enough to take it from there. As the young people became more and more conscious of American music, "modern" dances were held upstairs in the Town Hall while *La Charmarita* and other Portuguese dances went on downstairs.

Although Portuguese dances are gay, the musical form that is at the very core of the Portuguese spirit — the *fado* — is haunting, melodious and tremendously sad. The singers are called *fadistas.* According to tradition they always dress in black and wear black shawls. The word *fado* means "fate," and in the songs lost loves are wept for, lost illusions deplored and the inevitability of death lamented. The music is bitter-sweet, melancholy and almost always in a minor key.

Among the customs and beliefs that were brought here in past years, there were many superstitions which, even today, evoke a kind of scary delight, particularly around All Hallow's Eve or Halloween, the night before All Saints' Day. Many kinds of witches and spirits inhabited Portugal and the islands — *benzedores* and *imaginarios, magicos, agoureiros, bruxas* and *feiticeiras.* You could avoid their evil influences by opening a pair of scissors in the form of a cross, and Portuguese literature abounds with legends, charms and incantations in which they play a major role. Then, of course, everyone knew that if your hair started to fall out you had only to cut off a lock of it on St. John's Night and bury it under a quick-growing plant, such as a pumpkin vine, and you'd soon have luxuriant tresses again.

Perhaps the best summation of the Portuguese of Provincetown was written by Mary Heaton Vorse, known locally as "Mother Vorse," in her book *Of Time and the Town,* published in 1942.

"The daring of Portuguese fishermen," she said, "is part of Provincetown's legend. The interwoven strands of Portuguese and New England culture are so close you cannot tell where one begins and the other ends. The same boy who shouts in Portuguese to his father on the wharves talks in a New England accent about the 'habbor' the next moment. Good looks, gaiety, daring are their inheritance, yet they have the conservatism of the Latin."

The Portuguese, Mrs. Vorse concluded, are "woven into the fabric" of Provincetown, "whose discreet white houses shelter a South European population."

The richness of the Portuguese culture has been subtly and gracefully added to the American tradition, as flavoring is added to a stew, and not the least important part is their food.

On to the
Kitchen

If America paid no other tribute to those who came here from
Portugal, she should be everlastingly grateful for the introduction
of Portuguese food. These recipes are culinary collectors' items and
are not easy to come by. I have amassed mine over a period of years
from a variety of sources. Unfortunately, this really superlative cuisine is relatively unknown in most of the United States, except coastal
New England where many Portuguese dishes have been assimilated
and are almost as native now as baked beans and clam chowder.

At most Cape Cod hamburger stands you will find "linguiça rolls" on the menu. Linguiça is a Portuguese sausage with a very distinctive flavor that seems to stem principally from the addition of paprika, vinegar and spices to the meat mixture, plus the fact that the sausage is smoked. Chouriço is a first cousin to linguiça, the principal difference between the two sausages being a matter of seasoning. Chouriço is usually spicier, due to the addition of hot red pepper. Both are "hard" sausages, similar in texture to Italian peperoni or salami.

Linguiça *does* make a difference in Portuguese cooking; chouriço may be dispensed with if it is not readily available, and linguiça substituted in any recipe which calls for it. So it is worth an effort to obtain linguiça. If you can't find it in your local store, you may be able to prevail upon the manager to order it for you. If not, you can order it yourself by mail from either Gaspar's Linguiça Company, Inc., 540 Dartmouth Street, South Dartmouth, Massachusetts 02738, or the New Bedford Linguiça Company, manufacturer of Fragozo Products, 56 Davis Street, New Bedford, Massachusetts 02746. Linguiça, incidentally, is probably the only item really needed in Portuguese cooking which may not be readily found in every supermarket across the United States.

Just as most people no longer make their own breakfast sausage or frankfurters, so very few make their own linguiça today. But not so long ago, this was done by many Portuguese-American families in the environs of Cape Cod.

Autumn was the time of harvest and the time to slaughter the the pigs. It was a community affair; a kind of fiesta with everyone, young and old, taking part. The pork was cut into roasts and chops and preserved in brine before refrigerators became commonplace. Today one of the most delicious of all the Portuguese pork dishes features chops which have been marinated for several days to achieve the same effect and flavor.

The extra bits of meat were diced and mixed with vinegar, spices and lots of paprika, the precise mixture depending upon a family's own particular taste. Some added garlic, some preferred to leave it out. When the meat mixture was well seasoned, it was stuffed into sausage casings and hung in the family smokehouse where wonderful aromas would penetrate the sausages, giving them that "different" flavor. After a few days in the smokehouse, the linguiça was stored for use in the months to come. It keeps very well, by the way. I store it in the meat bin of my refrigerator and it seems to last indefinitely.

If you can't wait to buy linguiça before trying a recipe which calls for it, a good facsimile can be achieved by substituting Italian peperoni which is available almost everywhere. You need the sausage peperoni that is about an inch or more in diameter, and you use half the amount of peperoni that the recipe requires of linguiça. If the recipe calls for half a pound of linguiça, substitute one quarter of a pound of peperoni and add, *in addition to the listed ingredients,* two teaspoons of vinegar, half a bay leaf, two teaspoons of paprika and about three good dashes of liquid smoke. Bottles of liquid smoke, which are available in food specialty stores and sometimes even in supermarkets, usually have shaker tops for convenience. Although this is a strong substance, it is surprising how much of it a dish will absorb before approximating the taste of linguiça. The best course is to start out with one dash, then sample as you go along until you have the desired amount. If you have never tasted linguiça it is obviously impossible to be exact about this; another reason why you should try the real thing at least once!

The result of this substitute method will still not taste the same as linguiça because the seasonings in the two sausages are quite different; peperoni, as the name implies, is the "peppery-er" of the two. But you will obtain a very good dish that is quite Portuguese in flavor. Also, the substitution should be made only in those recipes where linguiça is one ingredient of several; that is, a soup, stew or something in which a variety of things simmer together. In recipes where linguiça stands alone — and there are not all that many of them — the genuine product does have to be used.

As for cooking utensils, you need a large, deep pot because some of the soup recipes make a large quantity. Don't worry about left-overs — if there are any, they can be frozen for future use. You will also need a sturdy wooden spoon for stirring and a fairly large casserole, perhaps a two-quart size, for some recipes. I prefer the earthenware types, and my own favorite for such dishes as *bacalhau* is a glazed stoneware oval that is perhaps twelve inches long and three inches deep.

In the First Place:

PORTUGUESE SOUPS

Portuguese food really begins with soup; rich, sustaining soup that is so good one feels that if he hasn't made a meal of it he should have! Traditionally the Portuguese are not before-dinner cocktail drinkers, and so hors d'oeuvres as such play a scant part in their cuisine. At a Portuguese-American cocktail party, the tidbits are apt to have an American accent. Sometimes there is something Portuguese-flavored, but this is usually achieved by making dishes such as "pigs in blankets" or "stuffed clam casserole" in smaller sizes. Adaptations for cocktail-time delicacies such as these will be given with the recipes later in the book.

Although you will see "Portuguese soup" advertised on restaurant menus, there is no such thing as one Portuguese soup. It is a highly individual dish, the sole common factor being that most contain linguiça.

A hearty soup with fresh Portuguese bread — or Italian or French bread when the real thing is not available — makes a substantial lunch or Sunday night supper. If you intend to have one of these soups as a prelude to a meal, limit each serving to a single cup and refuse seconds! It is so filling that, unless you do, no one will have an appetite left for the next course.

My first attempt at making the famous *caldo verde,* which literally means "green broth," was a disaster. Often called "kale soup," this is what many people insist is *the* Portuguese soup. My recipe called for two pounds of kale. In my ignorance, I simply chopped it up in rather large pieces, cooked the whole thing and came out with a mass of greenery that would have defied even the most intrepid kale lover.

Actually kale should be chopped — but not minced — into fairly small pieces. Many Portuguese cooks today use frozen chopped kale, which is often available when the fresh product is not. I would recommend the frozen kale, at least the first time around. The pieces are just the right size for soup, and so provide a lesson as well as a convenience.

All of the vegetables that go into Portuguese soup, for that matter, should be cut fairly small to achieve a blending of ingredients rather than large, separate bites of different things, but it is often a matter of personal taste. You may discover that on one occasion you want chunks of potato that you can bite into; on another you may prefer it combined more discreetly with the other ingredients. The linguiça is normally sliced, but again one does not need to

be precise. The slices should be neither thick nor thin, but a happy medium.

Where recipes call for chick peas, pinto beans, kidney beans or any of the other "beans" that may be bought either dried or canned, I must admit that I take the easy way out and buy the canned product. If you prefer, you can soak and cook dried beans before adding them to the recipe.

MY FAVORITE PORTUGUESE SOUP

2 tablespoons olive oil
3 fresh tomatoes (or 1 cup
  canned tomatoes)
2 onions, diced
1 clove garlic, minced
3 stalks celery, diced
3 carrots, diced
3 potatoes, diced

¼ medium cabbage,
  shredded
1 cup chick peas, cooked
  or canned
½ pound linguiça, sliced
1 beef bouillon cube
salt and pepper

Sauté the tomatoes, onions and garlic in just enough olive oil to cover the base of the large, deep pot you are going to cook the soup in. Add the celery, carrots, potatoes, the shredded cabbage and the chick peas. Cover with water. Simmer for 10 minutes and add the linguiça. Crumble the bouillon cube into the soup and taste for seasoning. Add salt and pepper, if desired. Cover and simmer over a low heat for 1 to 2 hours, the longer the better. More water can be added if the liquid seems low. Like most such dishes, this is even more flavorful when warmed up the second day — if you can make it last that long! *Serves 4 to 6.*

PORTUGUESE SOUP II

2 pounds shank beef
with bone
1 large onion, diced
3 potatoes, diced

1 medium cabbage, cut in
small chunks
1 pound linguiça, sliced
salt and pepper

Cover the beef bone with water and simmer, covered, for about 2 hours, or until the meat is tender. Add the onions, potatoes, cabbage, linguiça, and salt and pepper to taste. Add more water to cover, if necessary. Cook over a low heat for 1 hour. Serve with Portuguese bread. *Serves 6 to 8.*

PORTUGUESE SOUP III

4 pounds pumpkin or
butternut squash
sugar
3 pounds lamb shoulder meat
1 cup chick peas, cooked or
canned

1 onion, diced
salt and pepper
3 potatoes, diced
½ pound elbow macaroni

Prepare the pumpkin or squash by cutting into bite-sized pieces and sprinkling them lightly with sugar to enhance the taste. Set aside. Place the lamb, chick peas, onion and seasonings in a large kettle and cover with water. Cover the pot and simmer for about 1½ hours or until the meat is tender. Add the potatoes and the pumpkin or squash. Cook until these are done but not mushy, about ½ hour. Add the macaroni and cook until it is tender. *Serves 8 to 10.*

PORTUGUESE SOUP IV

2 tablespoons olive oil
4 fresh tomatoes or 4 large
   canned tomatoes, drained
   and chopped
1 onion, diced
½ pound linguiça, sliced

2 carrots, diced
1 pound cabbage or kale,
   chopped
1 16-ounce can tomatoes
1 16-ounce can chick peas
salt and pepper

Sauté the chopped tomatoes and onion in enough olive oil to cover the bottom of a deep kettle. Add the linguiça, carrots, cabbage or kale and the can of tomatoes, plus enough water to cover. (The canned tomatoes give a slightly different flavor and more liquid.) Simmer, covered, for about 1 hour. Add the chick peas, salt and pepper to taste, and cook for at least an additional 15 minutes. A longer cooking time over low heat enhances the flavor. *Serves 4 to 6.*

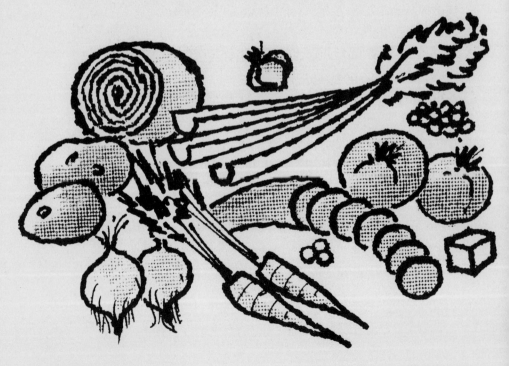

PORTUGUESE SOUP V

Soup bones or bones from
leftover pork or beef roast
Lean bacon, 3 or 4 slices or a
2-inch wide chunk
Lima or kidney beans, cooked
or canned

Finely diced vegetables:
carrots, onions, cabbage,
celery, turnip tops, young
mustard greens or beet tops
Diced linguiça or frankfurters
salt and pepper

This is a recipe in which you may let your imagination have full
rein. Begin by putting the bones in a large pot and covering them
with water. Add the lean bacon. Cover the pot and let the bones
and bacon simmer for about 1 hour. Remove the bones. To the liquid
stock add the vegetables — as many as you want, of whatever variety
you want. The only rule is to include at least two varieties of chopped
greens. Then add linguiça or diced frankfurters and any other leftover meat you wish. Salt and pepper to taste and let the brew simmer over a low heat for at least 1 additional hour. Serve with either
Portuguese cornbread or regular Portuguese bread. *The number of
people this recipe will feed depends on what you put into the pot.*

CALDO VERDE I
(Kale Soup)

1 pound fresh or 2 packages
  frozen chopped kale
4 potatoes, diced
1 onion, chopped

1 teaspoon salt
1 tablespoon bacon drippings
1 tablespoon olive oil
boiling water for scalding

Prepare the fresh kale by washing it thoroughly, making sure you get all the sand out, and then chopping it into fine pieces. Or take the easy way, which is every bit as good, and use the frozen variety. Set the kale aside in a pan of cold water. Boil the potatoes, onion and salt with the bacon drippings in 2½ quarts of water. When the potatoes are thoroughly cooked, mash them right in the pan, blending them into the broth. You only need to mash them coarsely with a fork and wooden spoon. Drain the kale and pour boiling water over it. Once it has been scalded, drain it again and add it to the potato and broth mixture. Salt, if necessary, and bring the soup to a boil, adding a tablespoon of olive oil. Cook over a low heat, uncovered, for about 15 minutes, stirring frequently. If it seems too thick, add a little extra boiling water. This is often served with chunks of Portuguese bread right in the bowl. *Serves 4 to 6.*

CALDO VERDE II

1 pound kidney, pinto or
    white beans, canned or
    cooked
1 pound fresh or 2 packages
    frozen chopped kale

1 pound linguiça, sliced
6 small potatoes, diced
salt and pepper

Put the beans, chopped kale and linguiça in a deep pot. Salt and pepper to taste, cover with water and cook over a slow heat for 1 hour. Add the potatoes and cook until they are tender. *Serves 8 to 10.*

CALDO VERDE III

1 pound chouriço (or
    linguiça if it is not
    available), sliced
1 cup pinto beans, cooked or
    canned
1 large onion, diced

1 pound fresh kale or 2
    packages frozen chopped
    kale
1 tablespoon vinegar
2 cups potatoes, diced
salt and pepper

Put the chouriço, beans, onion, chopped kale, vinegar, and salt and pepper in a large pot with 2½ quarts of water. Bring to a boil, then cover and simmer for 2 to 3 hours. Add the potatoes and continue cooking until they are tender. If the liquid seems low, add more hot water.   *Serves 8 to 10.*

COUVRES

2 cups chick peas, cooked or
   canned
½ pound linguiça, sliced
salt and pepper

1 pound fresh or 2 packages
   frozen chopped kale
6 small potatoes, cut in
   eighths

This is also a kale soup and a great favorite with Portuguese fisher-men. If you are using fresh kale, prepare and chop it as mentioned above. Put all the ingredients in a deep pot, cover with water and simmer, with the pot covered, for 1 to 2 hours. *Serves 6.*

PHYLLIS' KALE SOUP

1 large onion, sliced
1 beef shin bone
1 pound stew beef, cubed
1 pound chuck steak (one
   piece)
½ pound linguiça, sliced
1 pound fresh or 2 packages
   frozen chopped kale

4 potatoes, quartered
½ medium cabbage, cut in
   thirds
1 16-ounce can pinto
   or horticultural beans
salt and pepper

Use a large, heavy kettle for this. Put in about 2 quarts of water or enough to cover all the ingredients when added to the pot. Then add the onion, shin bone, stew beef and chuck steak. Simmer slowly for 1 hour. Add the linguiça and simmer for another 30 minutes, adding a little extra water if the liquid seems to be getting low. Add the chopped kale, potatoes, cabbage, beans, salt and pepper to taste, and simmer for 2 more hours.

Remove the chuck steak, stew beef and shin bone with a slotted spoon, and put the meat on a platter. Serve the soup and then let each person help himself to as much of the meat as he wishes, either putting it in the soup or eating it separately.   *Serves 10 to 12.*

PHYLLIS' BEAN SOUP

2-inch chunk of salt pork
1 medium onion, chopped
¼ teaspoon freshly ground
  nutmeg
1 tablespoon chopped parsley
  or parsley flakes

1 8-ounce can tomato sauce
1 16-ounce can pinto
  or horticultural beans
1½ teaspoons salt
½ pound macaroni

Cut the salt pork into thin slices and sauté until nicely browned. Add the onion and sauté until it is transparent. Add the nutmeg and parsley. Cook until the mixture is soft. Add the tomato sauce and 2 cups of water. Cover and cook slowly for 1½ to 2 hours. Then put the beans into a large kettle, and add 4 cups of water and the salt to them. Strain the sauce derived from the pork-onion-parsley mixture into this kettle on top of the beans. Put 3 or 4 ladles of the beans into the strainer and mash them through. Add the macaroni and simmer until it is done. *Serves 4 to 6.*

JOEL O'BRIEN'S PORTUGUESE SOUP

2 large onions, sliced
1 tablespoon olive oil
1 tablespoon butter or
   margarine
1 pound linguiça, sliced
4 potatoes, diced
2 16-ounce cans red kidney
   beans

2 cups dry red wine
1 pound fresh kale or 2
   packages frozen chopped
   kale
½ bay leaf
salt and pepper
cayenne pepper
1 heaping tablespoon sugar

Joel O'Brien has had a lifetime acquaintance with Provincetown and is an expert cook. His Portuguese soup has a different touch because he uses red wine in it. He also prefers to skin his linguiça, but says this is a matter of personal preference.

Sauté the onions in a deep pot in equal parts of oil and margarine or butter — enough to cover the pan and prevent the onions from burning. When the onions have started to become translucent, add the linguiça and let the two simmer together over a low fire until the onions are soft. Meanwhile, dice the potatoes, put them in a separate pan, cover them with water and parboil until they can be pierced but not broken with a fork. Drain them.

To the onion and linguiça mixture add 4 cups of water, the kidney beans, wine, kale, potatoes and bay leaf. As soon as the bay leaf flavor is detectable, remove it. (I never tasted it that much, but some people are very sensitive to the flavor of bay leaf.) Add salt and pepper to taste, a dash of cayenne for "character," and a heaping tablespoon of what Joel calls "that most misunderstood of all condiments," sugar. Let this mixture simmer over a slow fire for 1½ to 2 hours. Serve it with Portuguese bread and more red wine. Actually, Joel likes to make the soup the day before he intends to serve it, since it improves with some aging. *Serves 8 to 10.*

Something of Substance:

FISH, MEAT AND OTHER MAIN DISHES

Fish and Shellfish

The Portuguese call cod *o fiel amigo,* "faithful friend," and little wonder. This international fish, sometimes fresh but especially salted, is a basic element in the cuisine of Portugal and, for that matter, all of the Mediterranean countries. The word for codfish is *bacalhau* and, when blended with such accessories as onions, tomatoes, garlic and potatoes, it is superlative.

Although many of the recipes seem to have the same basic ingredients, or at least share a large number of them, there are subtle flavor variations. Many herbs and spices are used which blend with one another so that the result is a kind of harmony.

As might be expected the Portuguese make great stews and casseroles with fish and shellfish and like their soups, most of them are old family recipes. They make marveloüs complete meals when accompanied by Portuguese bread and *salada verde*.

BACALHAU I

2 pounds (2 wooden boxes)   ½ large can of pitted black
   salt cod   olives
6 potatoes, sliced   2 20-ounce cans tomatoes
4 onions, sliced   4 tablespoons olive oil
1 6-ounce jar pimientos   salt and pepper

Soak the cod overnight in cold water. Drain, rinse thoroughly in fresh cold water and drain again. Flake it into large segments. Slice the potatoes, onions, pimientos and olives and put each ingredient onto a separate piece of waxed paper or dish. Oil a large casserole, preferably glass or earthenware, and line it with a layer of fish. Cover this with a layer of potatoes, then layers of onions, pimientos, olives and tomatoes, strewing each across the surface. Repeat the layers, saving some of the pimientos and olives to decorate the top. Dribble the olive oil evenly over the top and sprinkle with salt and pepper. Cover the casserole and bake at 350° for 1½ hours. This is a flexible dish; you can turn the oven off, keep the casserole covered and it will hold until you are ready to serve it.

Serves 6 to 8.

BACALHAU II

2 pounds (2 wooden boxes)
  salt cod
½ cup olive oil
1 onion, chopped
1 green pepper, diced
4 cloves garlic, minced
1 cup celery, chopped

1 dozen fresh mushrooms,
  chopped
2 20-ounce cans tomatoes
1 cup dry white wine
½ cup sliced toasted
  almonds
salt and pepper

If toasted almonds are not available in your local store, buy sliced almonds instead. Spread them out on a cookie sheet and toast them in a 300° oven for 8 to 10 minutes until they are slightly brown. Watch them carefully so they do not get too brown.

Soak the codfish overnight in cold water. Drain, rinse thoroughly in fresh cold water and drain again. Separate the fish into large flakes. Heat the olive oil in a deep kettle and sauté the onions, green pepper, garlic and celery in it until they are soft. Add the mushrooms, tomatoes, wine, almonds, salt and pepper and simmer for 5 minutes, stirring constantly. Add the codfish and be sure that the sauce covers it completely. A little water may be added if necessary. Cover the kettle and cook over a low heat for about ½ hour without stirring the mixture. Be sure to have Portuguese bread to go along with this.   *Serves 6 to 8.*

GOMES DE SA

2 pounds (2 wooden boxes)
  salt cod
6 potatoes, parboiled and
  sliced
1 cup olive oil
6 onions, sliced
4 cloves garlic, minced
½ teaspoon thyme
½ cup parsley, chopped
1 bay leaf

½ teaspoon cumin seed
½ teaspoon black pepper
1 cup dry white wine
1 cup tomato juice
2 teaspoons Worcestershire
  sauce
¼ teaspoon tabasco sauce
½ cup bread crumbs
½ cup grated parmesan
  cheese

Gomes de Sa was a man whose name somehow long ago became associated with this recipe. Soak the codfish overnight in cold water. Drain, rinse thoroughly in fresh cold water and drain again. Cut into 2-inch pieces. Parboil and slice the potatoes. Heat the oil in a deep kettle and sauté the onions and garlic in it until they are soft. Add the thyme, parsley, bay leaf, cumin and black pepper, stirring well. Next add the wine, tomato juice, Worcestershire sauce and tabasco and simmer for 5 minutes. Add the parboiled potatoes and fish and cook until the potatoes are tender, about 15 minutes. For added flavor, sprinkle the top of the dish with bread crumbs and parmesan cheese. Place in a 300° oven and cook for about 10 more minutes until the cheese is lightly browned.   *Serves 6 to 8.*

LISBON CODFISH BALLS

1 pound (1 box) salt codfish	dash of nutmeg
3 potatoes, diced	3 egg yolks
1 onion, chopped	3 egg whites
1 teaspoon parsley	olive oil
dash of pepper	

Soak the cod overnight in cold water. Drain, rinse in fresh cold water and drain again. Place the fish and potatoes in a deep saucepan, cover with water and cook until the potatoes are tender. Drain and mash the potatoes and fish together. Add the onion, parsley, pepper and nutmeg, and blend in slightly beaten egg yolks. Beat the egg whites until stiff and fold into the mixture. Put about 2 inches of olive oil in the bottom of a deep kettle and heat until a cube of bread quickly starts to turn golden brown when dropped into it. Drop the codfish mixture in by the tablespoon and fry carefully, turning with a long-handled fork, until the codfish balls are golden brown. Do 6 or 7 balls at a time and keep them warm in the oven on a heat-proof platter lined with paper towels. *Yields about 30 codfish balls.*

VINHO D'ALHOS

1 cup wine vinegar

3 cloves garlic, crushed

1 teaspoon cumin seed

dash of cayenne pepper

1 cup dry red wine

1 teaspoon salt

⅛ teaspoon saffron

2 pounds white fish filets

olive oil

Probably the best of all the fish dishes is *vinho d'alhos*. The *vinho d'alhos* is actually the mixture in which the fish marinates before cooking. *Vinho* means wine; *alhos* means garlic. Filets of almost any white fish may be used for this dish with equally good results. The only problem is that after tasting it you may never again want to eat fish prepared in any other way!

Combine all ingredients except the fish and oil. Stir this mixture well. Oil a large casserole, preferably glass or earthenware, and lay the fish filets close together across the bottom of it. Cover the fish with the marinade mixture, cover the casserole and let stand for several hours or overnight in the refrigerator, turning the fish once. The fish will absorb the red color of the wine and the wine vinegar to some extent. If you would prefer to keep it white, white vinegar and a dry white wine may be used quite satisfactorily; but the flavor is not as tangy.

When ready to cook the fish, liberally coat a large skillet with olive oil. Let the fish filets drain on a paper towel while the oil heats. Sear them on each side, reduce heat to medium-low and let them cook for about 20 minutes, or until the filets flake and are nicely done. Usually the fish soaks up quite a bit of the marinade and, in any event, I do not keep the leftover marinade for future use, as the wine and vinegar flavors tend to evaporate. *Serves 6.*

VINHO D'ALHOS II

2 pounds white fish filets
ground cumin
1 quart wine vinegar
3 cloves garlic, minced

2 teaspoons salt
⅓ cup pickling spices
2 tablespoons sugar
olive oil

Rub the fish filets with the cumin and place them in a large, oiled casserole. Mix the other ingredients and pour them over the fish, adding enough water to cover. Let this marinate in the refrigerator for 2 days. Drain the fish on paper towels. Sear on both sides in hot oil, reduce heat to medium-low and fry for about 20 minutes or until it gently flakes. *Serves 6.*

ASSADURAS DE PEIXE
(Fish Kabobs)

4 to 5 pounds large fresh or
   frozen fish filets
4 cloves garlic, crushed
1 teaspoon paprika
2 cups water

1 teaspoon crushed red
   peppers
1 cup wine vinegar
2 crushed bay leaves

If frozen fish is used, thaw first: haddock is preferred in this recipe. Combine the garlic, paprika, water, red peppers, vinegar and bay leaves to make the marinade. Pour it over the filets and let the fish sit for one hour. Drain and save the marinade. Cut the filets into long strips about 1 inch wide. Carefully wind them on skewers, making sure they are well secured in several places. Place them on a charcoal grill about 4 inches above the coals, or under your broiler. Cook for about 15 minutes, or until the fish flakes easily, turning often and brushing with the reserved marinade. The fish should be golden brown when it is done.

If you can obtain Portuguese rolls, split them and serve the fish in them. If not, serve in preheated frankfurter rolls. *Serves 8.*

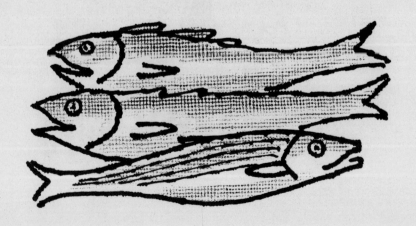

PORTUGUESE-STYLE BAKED FISH

3- to 4-pound whole fish

Stuffing

6 slices white bread

2 tablespoons olive oil

1 large onion, finely chopped

1 tablespoon white vinegar

salt and pepper

Sauce

2 cloves garlic, minced

½ cup white vinegar

½ cup water

salt and pepper

dash of saffron

Make the sauce by combining the above ingredients and stirring well. Set aside. To make the stuffing, first soak the bread in a little water and squeeze out the excess. Heat the olive oil and add the moist bread to it, along with the onion, vinegar, salt and pepper. Stir the mixture constantly as it fries to be sure that it is evenly browned and well blended. Stuff the fish with this mixture, then either sew up the opening or pin it closed. With a sharp knife, make three slits diagonally along each side of the body, each about 2 inches long. Place the fish in an oiled baking dish and pour the sauce over it. Bake at 350° for 1 hour. Remove it to a heated serving platter. Thicken the pan gravy with a little flour and pass it in a side dish to be spooned over the fish. *Serves 6.*

MOHLE

6 sliced onions
4 sliced green peppers
¼ cup olive oil
2 cups peeled tomatoes

1 tablespoon white or wine
  vinegar
1 teaspoon cumin seed
2 cloves garlic, crushed
⅛ teaspoon saffron

This is a Portuguese sauce which is served hot over cold fish or meat. It is especially good with roast beef or pork. The sauce itself is served hot or leftovers can be heated in it. Plain boiled rice goes nicely as a side dish.

Fry the onions and green peppers in the olive oil. Add the tomatoes and the seasonings and simmer until thick. If the mohle gets too thick when heating it, a little water can be added. That's all there is to it! *Yields about one pint.*

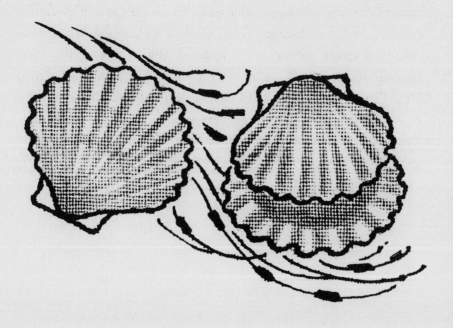

PORTUGUESE-STYLE SCALLOPS

2 pounds sea or bay scallops,
  fresh or frozen
½ cup flour
salt and pepper
6 tablespoons olive oil

2 cloves garlic, minced
2 or 3 tablespoons chopped
  parsley
2 or 3 tablespoons paprika

If the scallops are frozen, defrost them first. Pat dry with paper towels. Dust them lightly with the flour which has been seasoned with salt and pepper. Heat the olive oil and add the scallops and garlic. Cook them quickly, tossing lightly with a fork (use caution for they are tender) until they have browned evenly. Remove from heat. Lift the scallops out carefully with a slotted spoon. Toss them in a mixture of chopped parsley and paprika until lightly but evenly coated. *Serves 4.*

CALDEIRADA A PESCADORA
(Fisherman's Stew)

3 tablespoons olive oil
4 onions, sliced
3 cloves garlic, minced
½ bunch parsley, chopped
1 teaspoon coriander seeds
2 pounds white fish filets

6 potatoes, sliced
1 20-ounce can tomatoes
1 bay leaf
1 cup dry white wine
salt and pepper

Heat the olive oil in a deep pot. Add the onions, garlic, parsley, pepper and coriander. Cook until the onions are golden. Add the fish, potatoes, tomatoes, bay leaf, salt and wine and just enough water to cover. Cover and simmer for about 45 minutes.

Serves 6 to 8.

PORTUGUESE-STYLE CLAMS

2 quarts small quahogs or ½ pound linguiça, sliced
   cherrystone clams   2 onions, sliced

Place the clams in the sink and scrub the shells while fresh water runs over them continuously. When all possible sand is washed away, heat about 2 inches of fresh water to boiling in a deep kettle. Add the clams and scatter the linguiça and onions over them. Cover the kettle and steam over medium-high heat for 15 to 20 minutes. Lift the lid occasionally and peek. When the shells have opened, they should be done. Test one clam by tasting and if it is firm, but not hard, it is ready. You want to be sure that all the clams are done, which may take a bit longer depending on the depth of the pot. Serve with Portuguese bread and side dishes of oil and vinegar and melted butter. Dunk the clams in either the oil and vinegar or the butter. The broth, served in side cups, is delicious as an added "dunk" or a drink.

For this dish you may also use soft-shelled or steamer clams. They present more of a problem where sand is concerned, however. If they seem to be quite sandy, soak them in water sprinkled with cornmeal. For some mysterious reason, this causes the clams to disgorge their sand more efficiently. You may need to soak them for a few hours and change the water during the process. Once they are clean, proceed as you would with quahogs.

Check over the clams before you use them. The quahog shells should be tightly closed. The steamers should have their "necks" protruding, and if you touch those necks they should retract slightly, assuring that you still have a lively clam.

Serves 3 to 4, depending upon the appetites.

PORTUGUESE CLAM CASSEROLE

1 quart minced clams
1 pound linguiça, skinned
    and finely chopped
6 slices of bread, crumbled
1 medium onion, minced
2 teaspoons parsley, chopped

¼ teaspoon salt
¼ teaspoon black pepper
¼ teaspoon cayenne pepper
½ teaspoon garlic powder
1 egg, lightly beaten

If you are not about to dig your own clams Cape-Cod style, and then open them and grind the meat, buy fresh clams already minced from your local fish market or substitute an equal quantity of canned minced clams. Not even your best friend will be the wiser!

Mix the minced clams with the linguiça, bread, onion, parsley and seasonings. When this is well blended, add the egg and stir in thoroughly. Put the mixture into a two-quart, oiled casserole and bake at 350° for 30 minutes or until firm when knife-tested.

Serves 6.

A cocktail-time appetizer may be made with this mixture, but when I use it for that purpose I add about 2 teaspoons of olive oil and a full teaspoon (instead of the 1/2 teaspoon) of garlic powder.

If you can obtain cherrystone-sized quahog shells 2 to 3 inches in diameter, scrub them out and pack the mixture into them, rounding each one off. Sprinkle with flavored bread crumbs and a little paprika and bake at 375° for 20 minutes. If you cannot obtain the shells, bake the mixture in small, oiled tart tins or miniature muffin pans for the same length of time and serve on rounds of toast.

Makes approximately 24 to 30 appetizers.

Meat and other Main Dishes

The distinctive touch that makes these meat dishes "Portuguese" is vinegar. Saying this may give the wrong impression, especially to people who don't like vinegar, but in Portuguese cuisine, it becomes a very subtle thing. Usually only a tablespoon of it is used in an entire recipe (except when making a marinade), and more often than not it is added toward the end of the cooking period. You won't recognize the taste as vinegar, so don't omit it or try to substitute anything else; it is essential to success.

PORTUGUESE PORK CHOPS

6 to 8 pork chops
2 tablespoons sugar
2 cups dry white wine
¼ cup whole mixed
   pickling spices

2 cups cider vinegar
2 teaspoons salt
2 cloves garlic, minced
½ teaspoon ground cumin
olive oil

Arrange the pork chops in a lightly oiled casserole, preferably glass or earthenware. Mix the remaining ingredients (except the olive oil) and pour this marinade over the chops. Add enough water to cover. Cover the casserole, place it in the refrigerator and let the chops bask in this marinade for 3 days, turning them occasionally. Remove them and discard the marinade. Pat the chops dry with paper towels and fry them for about 30 minutes, or until they are thoroughly cooked, in just enough oil to cover the bottom of a large skillet. This is one of the most famous Portuguese meat dishes and it justly deserves the reputation. Serve with rice and *salada verde*.

Serves 4 to 6.

FOLAR
(Meat Pie)

Dough

1 package active dry yeast
  or 1 yeast cake

¾ cup sugar

1 pinch of ginger

⅓ cup warm water

1 cup scalded milk

½ cup butter or margarine

3 well-beaten eggs

1 medium potato, mashed

5 cups flour

1 teaspoon salt

½ stick melted butter for
  top of dough

1 beaten egg for top of folar

Filling

3 pounds lean pork, cubed

1 tablespoon pickling spices

1 cup wine vinegar

1 cup red wine

½ pound linguiça, sliced

½ pound bacon, diced

Folar is a festive dish, a kind of meat pie quite different from anything else and very, very good. My original recipe made enough to serve an entire fiesta so, in order to make the project more practicable, I turned to a Portuguese friend who is a professional chef and who, happily, likes to experiment with things culinary in his time off.

Thanks to Jim Arruda, the following recipe makes one folar. To accomplish it, he says, took "about seven hours of work, but it was worth it. The dough is delicious and quite sweet. The recipe makes a little too much dough, but it is so good that I made some biscuits with the leftovers. I've also used this dough for pancakes, which I made about 5 inches in diameter and about ⅛ inch thick, pressing some slices of fried linguiça into them and then baking them at 350° until they are nice and brown (12 to 15 minutes)."

The folar is made of three layers of dough which are stacked together like a layer cake with a meat filling between each layer and then baked. Jim says that his finished product was about 7 inches high "and so beautiful I didn't want to cut it."

Marinate the pork in the pickling spices, wine and vinegar for 24 hours, being sure that all surfaces of the meat are treated. When ready to cook, drain the meat and fry along with the bacon and linguiça until brown. Set aside.

Prepare the dough fairly early in the morning of the day you intend to make the folar so that it has ample opportunity to rise. Mix the yeast with a teaspoon of the sugar, the ginger and warm water and set aside. In a large bowl, mix the scalded milk with the butter, eggs, the remaining sugar and mashed potato. Add the yeast mixture, making sure that the milk and potato mixture is warm but not hot, or the yeast will not work.

Mix the flour with the salt in a separate large container and gradually add the liquid mixture to it. Mix well, turn out on a floured surface and knead until smooth. Brush the top of the dough with melted butter, cover it and let it rise until smooth, about 2 to 3 hours. This is a rich, heavy dough which may take a bit longer to rise than an ordinary dough.

Divide the dough into thirds. Roll it out in circles about ¼ inch thick and approximately 9 inches in diameter. It is important that the layers of dough are kept quite thin because they rise considerably when cooking. Grease and flour a fairly deep (about 3 inches) 9-inch round baking pan. Place a round of dough in it and arrange one half of the meat mixture over the top. Cover with another round of dough and cover it with the balance of the meat, then top with the third circle of dough. Cover and let the folar rise until double in bulk, again about 2 to 3 hours. Brush the top with a beaten egg, place it in a preheated 325° oven and bake for approximately 1 hour, or until nicely browned. *Serves 8 to 10.*

PORTUGUESE POT ROAST

5 pounds lean, boneless beef
   roast—bottom round,
   chuck or rump
olive oil
salt and pepper
1 20-ounce can Italian-style
   tomatoes

4 onions, sliced
6 carrots, cut in large pieces
1 large turnip, cut in large
   pieces
6 whole medium potatoes
2 tablespoons white or wine
   vinegar

Place the meat in a deep pot with a small amount of olive oil, sprinkle with salt and pepper and sear on all sides. Add the tomatoes,
onions and enough water to cover. Let the meat simmer slowly
for 2 to 3 hours, or until it is reasonably tender when pierced with
a fork. Add the carrots, turnips, potatoes and vinegar. Cover and
simmer until the vegetables are tender. If the liquid is low, additional
water may be added, but be sparing. You may never wish to
make any other kind of pot roast! *Serves 6 to 8.*

PORTUGUESE LAMB STEW

2 pounds stewing lamb, cut
in 2-inch cubes
½ cup cider vinegar
3 cloves garlic, minced
salt and pepper
2 tablespoons bacon fat
2 onions, sliced
4 stalks celery, diced

2 teaspoons poultry seasoning
2 bay leaves
3 large potatoes, diced
1 cup elbow macaroni
1 20-ounce can Italian-style
tomatoes
paprika
1 20-ounce can yellow lima
beans

Combine the lamb, vinegar, garlic, salt and pepper together in a large glass bowl, cover and let stand overnight. Drain. Heat bacon fat in a large deep kettle, add the drained meat and brown on all sides. Add the onions and celery and sauté until the onions are golden. Add 4 cups of water, the poultry seasoning, bay leaves and additional salt and pepper if desired. Bring to a boil and then simmer, covered, for 1½ hours. Add the potatoes. Again bring the stew to a boil, lower the temperature and simmer for about 20 minutes. Add the macaroni, lima beans, tomatoes and paprika and cook for 10 minutes more, or until the macaroni is tender. *Serves 6 to 8.*

PORTUGUESE-STYLE CHICKEN

1 large onion, sliced
2 cloves garlic, minced
2 tablespoons butter or
  margarine
2 bay leaves
1 chicken bouillon cube

salt and pepper
2 tablespoons white or cider
  vinegar
1½ cups chicken broth
1 large frying chicken, cut up

Sauté the onion and garlic in the butter, add the other seasonings, including the bouillon cube, mix and add the chicken broth. Add the chicken and simmer, covered, for about 1 hour or until very tender. More broth may be added if necessary; the dish should be moist. Rice is a good accompaniment to this.   *Serves 4.*

CHICKEN BREASTS IN WINE

6 boned chicken breasts
2 tablespoons olive oil
½ cup chicken broth
3 onions, sliced
1 clove garlic, minced
½ teaspoon tarragon

½ cup port
2 tablespoons Madeira
1 cup sour cream
nutmeg
salt and pepper

Fry the chicken in the oil until it is almost done, about 20 minutes. Add the broth and simmer, covered, for 10 minutes. In a separate pan sauté the onions until they are golden. Add the other ingredients to them. Blend this sauce thoroughly and pour over the chicken. Season with salt, pepper and nutmeg to taste, and simmer for an additional 5 minutes. If you prefer, the chicken may be served separately and the sauce passed at the table.   *Serves 6.*

LINGUIÇA AND MACARONI

1 large onion, sliced
1 green pepper, sliced
2 cloves garlic, minced
1 pound linguiça, cut into
   1-inch chunks

olive oil
1 20-ounce can Italian-style
   tomatoes
1 pound elbow macaroni
salt and pepper

Sauté the onion, pepper, garlic and linguiça in enough olive oil to cover the bottom of a large, deep kettle. When the onions are golden, add the tomatoes. Add the macaroni, enough water to cover (it should be juicy) and let the mixture cook until the macaroni is done. Salt and pepper to taste. This is a hearty, filling dish. *Serves 4.*

PORTUGUESE QUISH
(Linguiça-cheese pie)

½ cup heavy cream
½ pound bacon, chopped
½ pound grated Sierra da
   Estrella cheese (Swiss
   cheese may be substituted)
1 tablespoon chopped chives
2 slightly beaten egg yolks

1 cup milk
2 tablespoons parsley,
   chopped
1 tablespoon onion, chopped
¼ pound linguiça, thinly
   sliced
1 9-inch pastry shell, unbaked

Preheat the oven to 350°. Combine all the ingredients except the linguiça and fill the pastry shell with the mixture. Sprinkle the slices of linguiça over the top and bake for 20 minutes, or until the filling is firm. This makes an excellent luncheon dish accompanied by *salada verde.* *Serves 4 to 6.*

GRÃO DE BICO
(Linguiça and chick peas)

1 pound linguiça, cut in 1-inch chunks	2 tablespoons vinegar
2 medium onions, chopped	4 16-ounce cans chick peas
	1 teaspoon salt

Grão de Bico is the Portuguese name for chick peas. For a Sunday night supper or similar occasion, this is one of the best dishes imaginable. If any is left over, it only improves with reheating.

Put the linguiça in a deep kettle, cover it with water and simmer for 15 minutes. Add the other ingredients and a little additional water if necessary. Let the mixture cook over a slow heat for at least an hour to give the flavors a chance to blend thoroughly.

I like to make this early in the day and then reheat it at serving time. A good soup may be made by following this recipe and then thinning it considerably with a stock made of half water and half beef bouillon. Also you can add ½ pound of elbow macaroni or noodles and cook until they are done. *Either dish serves 6 to 8.*

PORTUGUESE PIGS IN BLANKETS

1 pound bread dough	1 pound linguiça
(packaged or homemade)	olive oil

This may be served either as a luncheon dish or an appetizer by simply varying the amount of dough used and the size of the linguiça pieces. For the luncheon dish, cut the linguiça into 3- or 4-inch lengths and pinch off enough dough to wrap around each piece. For an appetizer, cut the linguiça into 1-inch lengths and measure the dough accordingly.

Fry the linguiça in olive oil until it is partially browned and some of the fat has been rendered out. Drain it on paper towels. Prepare the bread dough according to the package instructions. Pinch off pieces of it and wrap around the linguiça. Seal the edges by moistening them with a little water and pressing them together. Let the "pigs in blankets" rise until they have doubled in bulk, then bake at 375° until nicely browned, about 12 to 15 minutes for the appetizers and 25 to 30 minutes for the luncheon rolls.

Makes about 6 luncheon rolls or 12 to 15 appetizers.

LINGUIÇA ROLLS

1 pound linguiça, cut into
   small chunks

1 onion, minced
6 frankfurter rolls

It is very easy to make an at-home version of the popular linguiça rolls served at wayside stands throughout coastal New England. Cut the linguiça into chunks and fry with the onion until well browned. Try to obtain the "New England" type of frankfurter rolls if you can, the ones that are split down the center top. Divide the linguiça evenly among the rolls.   *Serves 6.*

FAVAS

2 16-ounce cans favas or dried
   lima beans
2 to 3 garlic cloves, minced
1 teaspoon paprika
½ cup olive oil

2 to 3 chopped onions
1 tablespoon crushed red
   pepper
2 teaspoons parsley, chopped
1 tablespoon cider vinegar

This dish is a Portuguese favorite. Favas are large members of the lima bean family and may be bought either dried or canned. If not obtainable, use the canned dried lima beans, or soak and cook your own dried limas and use an equal amount.

Put all the ingredients together in a deep pot, adding the vinegar last. Cover the pot and let the mixture simmer slowly for about 30 minutes. Then let the pot stand on the back of the stove for several hours so that the flavors can blend. Reheat at serving time.

      Serves 6.

SALADA VERDE

⅓ small head Boston lettuce ¼ cup lemon juice
½ head chicory salt and pepper
½ head romaine 1 tomato, sliced
escarole, if desired black olives, for garnish
watercress, to taste 1 red onion, sliced, for garnish
¼ cup olive oil

A good green salad is the perfect accompaniment for any Portuguese meal — along with fresh Portuguese bread and a bottle of wine, of course. Such a salad may be made by using a combination of Boston lettuce, chicory, romaine and escarole, or similar greens, plus a bunch of watercress, washed and de-stemmed.

For the dressing, whisk together the olive oil and lemon juice (the bottled variety works perfectly well). Add a liberal quantity of salt and some freshly ground black pepper. Toss the greens lightly with the dressing, arrange on a platter and garnish with a sliced tomato, ripe olives and thin slices of red onion for color. *Serves 4.*

The Staffs of Life:

PORTUGUESE BREADS

You need only smell Portuguese bread baking once and you will be captive to it. It is fragrant and yeasty, with a crisp crust. Usually the loaves are round, occasionally oblong, but always delicious. The Portuguese are inclined to serve their bread plain or with butter rather than heating it or treating it with garlic. It has a water base, so it dries out easily if it is overheated or kept too long. Keeping it, however, is seldom a problem!

There is also a Portuguese sweet bread served either plain or toasted which makes a wonderful subsitute for coffee cake in breakfasts and brunches.

Then there are special breads such as *Massa Sovada* which is traditionally made at Easter, or the white bread made with a little cornmeal that is so very delicious and hails from St. Michael's in the Azores.

Portuguese bread is different from Italian or French bread, but if time doesn't permit baking a loaf, or if it isn't available where you live, you may substitute one of these and it will blend very nicely with your Portuguese main dish. But another time, try the real thing.

PORTUGUESE BREAD

2 tablespoons sugar
2½ teaspoons salt
6 tablespoons vegetable
   shortening
1 cup scalded milk or boiling
   water

1 package active dry yeast or
   1 yeast cake
1 cup warm water
6 cups flour

Water gives this bread a more traditional, coarse texture. Milk gives it a finer texture. Either way it is very good. Scald the milk if you are going to use it. Then stir the sugar, salt and shortening into the milk or boiling water. Cool to lukewarm. Meanwhile, dissolve the yeast in 1 cup warm water and stir into the first mixture. (The temperature of the "warm" water should be about 110° for active dry yeast and not quite so warm for compressed yeast cakes, about 85°.) Add 3 cups of flour and beat until smooth. Add the remaining flour a little at a time, blending completely. Turn the dough out onto a lightly floured board and knead until elastic, adding a little more flour if necessary. Place the dough in a large greased bowl, cover with a towel and put in a warm place where it can rise until doubled in size. Usually this takes about 1 hour. Punch down the dough to get rid of any air bubbles and divide in half. Shape each half into a round loaf about 8 inches across. Place the loaves in greased 8-inch round pans (cake pans will do), cover and let rise in a warm place for another hour, or until doubled in size. Bake in a hot 400° oven for about 50 minutes. *Yields 2 loaves.*

ST. MICHAEL'S BREAD

1 package active dry yeast or
  1 yeast cake
2 cups warm water
1 tablespoon sugar

2 tablespoons vegetable
  shortening
½ cup white cornmeal
1 tablespoon salt
5½ cups flour

Dissolve the yeast in ¼ cup warm water and add the sugar. Melt the shortening in the remaining 1¾ cups of warm water and mix with the yeast. Mix the cornmeal, salt and flour, then gradually add that mixture to the liquid. Turn the dough onto a lightly floured board and knead until elastic, adding more flour if necessary. Put the dough in a greased bowl, cover and let rise in a warm place until doubled in size. Grease 2 9-inch pie pans and sprinkle with some extra cornmeal. Punch down the dough to get rid of any air bubbles. Divide the dough in half and form into round loaves each about 8 inches across. Place them in the pans, cover and let rise again until doubled in size. Cut a cross on the top of each loaf with a sharp knife. Brush the surfaces with milk. Bake at 350° for 50 minutes.

Yields 2 loaves.

PÃO DOCE
(Sweet Bread)

1 pint milk, scalded

2 packages active dry yeast
   or 2 yeast cakes

¼ cup warm water

8 to 9 cups flour

1½ tablespoons salt

4 eggs

1½ cups sugar

⅛ pound melted butter

Scald the milk and set it aside. Let the eggs and other ingredients reach room temperature before using them. Dissolve the yeast in the warm water. Sift the flour and salt together into a large pan. Beat the eggs in a separate bowl, add the sugar and beat well, then add the melted butter and the yeast mixture. When thoroughly mixed, gradually add 8 cups of the flour to this batter, alternating it with the milk. Be sure that the milk has cooled to lukewarm before adding it; if it is too hot, it will stop the yeast action. When the dough is stiff, turn it out onto a lightly floured board and knead until smooth and satiny — about 8 to 10 minutes. Add the remaining cup of flour only if it seems necessary. Shape the dough into a smooth ball, grease the top, cover and let it rise until doubled in bulk. This is a heavy, rich dough, and so will take longer to rise than regular bread, the length of time depending upon the temperature. Try to find a spot where it is about 80°. Punch down the dough to get rid of any air bubbles and let it rise again until doubled. Then divide it into 3 loaves, shaping each into a flattened round. Place them in well-greased 9-inch pie or cake pans, cover and let rise a third time until doubled. Bake at 400° for about 40 minutes.

Yields 3 loaves.

MASSA SOVADA
(Portuguese Easter Bread)

1 cup milk, scalded

2 packages active dry yeast
or 2 yeast cakes

¼ cup warm water

3 eggs, well beaten

1 cup sugar

½ cup butter, melted

1 teaspoon lemon flavoring

5 cups flour

1 teaspoon salt

raw eggs in shells
(optional)

The addition of a raw egg on the top of each loaf is an old Portuguese custom still followed by many families. It is, some say, symbolic of the joyous Easter season, of fertility or of the Resurrection itself. You can add as many eggs to the top as you wish. In fact, there are often many included — one for each child, since children consider them a great treat. This traditional Easter bread also makes a wonderful gift.

Scald the milk and set it aside. Dissolve the yeast in the warm water. Beat the eggs, then add the dissolved yeast to them. Add the sugar, then the melted butter and the flavoring. Gradually stir in the flour and salt. Turn the dough out onto a lightly floured board and knead until it is very smooth and satiny, about 20 minutes. Place in a greased bowl, grease the top, cover and let rise until doubled in bulk. This will take from 2 to 3 hours. Punch the dough down and divide into 2 round loaves. Place each in a buttered 9-inch round cake or pie pan. Cover each and let them rise again until they are doubled.

Now comes the optional touch which is traditionally Portuguese. Wash the raw eggs in cold water. Scoop an egg-shaped amount of dough from the top of each loaf. Into this hollow carefully place the whole egg in its shell. Roll out the removed dough and place strips of it over each egg in the form of a cross. Brush the tops of the loaves with milk for a glaze and bake in a 350° oven for about 40 minutes or until golden brown.

The bread is served either plain or with sweet butter. Eat the egg or not, as you wish; it is simply hard boiled, or in this case, hard baked! *Yields 2 loaves.*

BROA
(Portuguese Cornbread)

1½ cups white cornmeal pulverized until fine	1 package active dry yeast or 1 yeast cake
1½ teaspoons salt	1 teaspoon sugar
1 cup boiling water	¼ cup lukewarm water
4 teaspoons olive oil	2 cups flour

The cornmeal should preferably be pulverized in a blender until fine. Combine 1 cup of the cornmeal, the salt and boiling water and blend until smooth. Stir in a tablespoon of olive oil and let the mixture cool until lukewarm. Dissolve the yeast and sugar in the lukewarm water. Set aside in a warm place until the yeast has doubled in volume. Stir this into the cornmeal mixture. Gradually add the remaining cornmeal and 1 cup of flour, stirring well. Form the dough into a ball, place in a greased bowl, cover with a towel and set in a warm place until the dough has doubled in bulk. Coat a 9-inch pie pan with olive oil. Turn the dough out onto a floured surface, punch down and knead for 5 minutes, adding as much of the remaining flour as you can, until it is firm but not stiff. Shape into a round, flattened loaf, place in the greased pan, cover with a towel and let it double in bulk again. Bake at 350° for 40 minutes, or until the top is golden. *Yields 1 loaf.*

MALASSADAS
(Portuguese Fried Dough)

1 cup scalded milk
½ cup sugar
1 teaspoon salt
½ cup butter
1 package active dry yeast
  or 1 yeast cake

¼ cup lukewarm water
2 eggs, slightly beaten
5 to 6 cups flour
corn or vegetable oil
granulated sugar for finishing

Scald the milk and add the sugar, salt and butter to it. Sprinkle the yeast into the lukewarm water and let it stand for 5 minutes. Stir until dissolved. Add the yeast mixture and eggs to the milk. Gradually add the flour, beating with a wooden spoon until it is too stiff to beat further. Place the dough on a lightly floured board and knead until smooth and elastic. Form it into a ball. Lightly grease a bowl and place the dough in it. Turn the dough over in the bowl so that its whole surface has a coating of the grease. Cover and set in a warm place to rise until doubled in bulk, about 1 hour. Lightly grease your palms and fingers. Break off — don't cut — a handful of dough at a time. Stretch it with your fingers into an oblong shape about the length of a cruller, but don't twist it. Fry in hot vegetable oil until golden brown on all sides. Test one to make sure it is done inside and not still gooey. Drain each "fritter" on a paper towel, sprinkle with granulated sugar and serve warm.

Yields about 12 malassadas.

Final Touches:

DESSERTS, CAKES AND COOKIES

Fruit is a favorite Portuguese dessert. So is the "flan" type of caramel custard which is found on Spanish, French and Italian menus as often as it is on Portuguese. It is always a smooth and soothing sort of dessert, especially after a spicy dinner. This is, perhaps, the reason for its widespread popularity. The Portuguese version has a special touch: it is flavored with that most famous of all Portuguese wines, port.

The Portuguese make a variety of delicious small cakes and cookies, some baked, some fried, all of them good accompaniments to an after-dinner glass of port or madeira.

PORTO PUDIM FLAN
(Port Custard Pudding)

1½ cups heavy cream   6 egg yolks
1½ cups milk   2 teaspoons port wine
¾ cup sugar

Blend the cream and milk in a heavy saucepan over high heat until small bubbles appear around the edges. Set aside. In a fairly large, heavy skillet, caramelize the sugar by stirring it over moderate heat until it melts and turns a golden brown. Immediately pour the hot cream and milk in a thin stream into the caramel, stirring constantly with a large spoon until the caramel is dissolved. Beat the egg yolks until well blended and pour slowly into the caramel cream mixture, stirring constantly. Stir in the port. Strain the mixture through a fine sieve and ladle it into either a 2-quart mold or 12 4-ounce custard cups. Place the mold or the cups in a pan containing enough hot water to reach about halfway up the sides. Bake at 350° for about 40 minutes, or until a knife inserted into the center comes out clean. Cool and refrigerate.

Unmold by running a sharp knife around the inner edge of the container, dipping the bottom briefly in hot water and then turning it upside down quickly onto a chilled serving plate. Hold the serving plate right over the face of the mold when you do this.

Serves 8 to 12.

PUDIM DE BANANAS
(Banana Pudding)

1 dozen bananas

3 ounces Madeira wine

3 tablespoons butter

1 cup sugar

6 eggs, well-beaten

Peel the bananas and cook them in a little water until they are soft. Put them through a sieve. Add the wine and butter and beat the mixture well. Add the sugar and eggs. Pour the mixture into a buttered soufflé dish or 2-quart casserole, and set in a pan of hot water. Bake, still in the hot water, at 350° for about 40 minutes, or until a knife inserted in the center comes out clean.   *Serves 8.*

PORTUGUESE WEDDING CAKES

1 cup butter	1 teaspoon almond flavoring
4 tablespoons powdered sugar	2½ cups flour, sifted
1 tablespoon grated lemon rind	50 blanched almonds
1 tablespoon water	additional powdered sugar for coating cakes

Although these are called "wedding cakes" they are really more like cookies. Cream the butter with the sugar, lemon rind and water. Add the almond flavoring. Mix in the flour — the easiest way to do this is to knead it in with your hands. Pinch off small pieces of dough, about the size of a large walnut, and press them flat. Put an almond in the center of each and roll the dough around it to make a little loaf. Place on a lightly greased and floured cookie sheet and bake at 350° for about 15 minutes until they are a light brown. Remove them from the cookie sheet and partially cool. Roll them in additional powdered sugar. Cool completely and again roll in sugar until there is a thick white coating. *Yields about 50 cookies.*

SONHOS
(Dreams)

Sonhos

1 cup water
½ teaspoon salt
1 teaspoon sugar

1 cup flour
8 eggs
vegetable oil or shortening

Syrup

1 cup sugar
1 cup water
cinnamon

almond flavoring
vanilla flavoring
powdered sugar for coating

Bring the water, salt and sugar to a boil. Add the flour all at once and stir constantly until the mixture is well blended and cooked — about 5 minutes. Cool. Add the eggs one at a time and work into the dough until well mixed, making a batter. Drop the batter into hot oil by the tablespoon, poking it with a fork so that it will expand and cook inside. Fry until golden brown. Drain on a paper towel and cool.

To make the syrup, boil the sugar and water together. Add the cinnamon, almond flavoring and vanilla to taste. Continue to boil, stirring constantly, until the mixture thickens and a syrup consistency is reached. Before serving, dip the sonhos in the syrup and then sprinkle with powdered sugar.   *Yields about 2 dozen sonhos.*

SUSPIROS
(Sighs)

3 egg whites   ½ teaspoon lemon juice
1 cup sugar

Beat the egg whites until they are very stiff. Gradually add the sugar and lemon juice. Line cookie sheets with either plain brown or waxed paper, Drop the mixture by heaping teaspoonfuls onto the cookie sheets, making little peaked mounds. Bake at 300° for 15 to 20 minutes, or until lightly browned and dry on the outside. Break one open to test: the inside should be soft but not "gooey."

These may also be tinted with a few drops of vegetable coloring, a nice touch at Christmas or other holiday occasions, and you can vary the basic recipe with any of the following additions:

1. Add ½ cup finely shredded blanched almonds and ¼ teaspoon almond flavoring, or

2. Add ¼ cup finely diced candied orange peel and ¼ teaspoon orange flavoring, or

3. Add ¼ cup finely diced dates and ¼ cup finely chopped walnuts with ½ teaspoon vanilla, or

4. Add ¼ cup finely chopped candied cherries.

Yields about 3 dozen suspiros.

BÔLOS

(Rolled Cakes)

1 package active dry yeast	1 cup vegetable shortening
or 1 compressed yeast cake	½ cup lukewarm orange
½ cup lukewarm water	juice
8 cups flour	1½ ounces brandy
1 teaspoon salt	1 cup butter
6 egg yolks	1½ cups granulated sugar

Dissolve the yeast in lukewarm water. Mix the flour, salt and egg yolks with softened shortening, orange juice and brandy. Add the yeast mixture and blend thoroughly. Set in a greased bowl and let rise in a warm place until doubled in size. Divide the dough in thirds for easier handling and roll it out paper-thin with a rolling pin, using no flour. It is best to do this on a pastry cloth or waxed paper.

Melt the butter and spread it thickly over the dough sections. Generously sprinkle each section with granulated sugar and roll up like a jelly roll. Be sure the rolls are tight. Cut each roll into slices about ¾-inch thick and place an inch apart on lightly greased cookie sheets. Bake at 325° for 30 minutes. Remove with a spatula while the bôlos are still warm.   *Yields about 10 dozen bôlos.*

TRUTAS

(Sweet-Potato Pastries)

Filling

1 pound sweet potatoes

1½ cups granulated sugar

½ grated lemon rind

1 teaspoon cinnamon

Dough

1 cup butter

5 cups flour

⅔ cup vegetable shortening

1 teaspoon salt

juice of four oranges

vegetable oil for frying

4 ounces brandy

powdered sugar

Boil the potatoes, peel and mash them. Add sugar and flavorings and cook together for about a minute, stirring constantly. Cool while preparing the dough.

Soften the butter and shortening, and blend in the orange juice, brandy, flour and salt. Mix together lightly as you would a pie crust. Roll out very thin and cut out circles with a 3-inch round cookie cutter or similar utensil. Place a spoonful of filling on each round, fold in half and crimp by pinching the edges. Fry in deep hot oil until golden brown. Drain and roll in powdered sugar.

Yields about 3 dozen trutas.

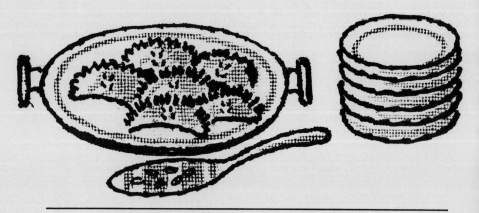

PORTUGUESE WALNUT SQUARES

Cake

½ cup softened butter or
  margarine
¾ cup packed light brown
  sugar
1 egg
½ teaspoon vanilla extract

2 tablespoons milk
5 tablespoons port wine
1½ cups finely chopped
  walnuts
6 tablespoons flour
½ teaspoon baking powder

Glaze

1 cup powdered sugar
dash of salt

1 tablespoon butter
1 tablespoon port

Cream the butter and sugar together for the cake. Add the egg and beat well. Then add the vanilla, milk, 2 tablespoons of the port and 1 cup of the nuts. Mix the flour and baking powder and add gradually to make a batter. Do not overbeat. Spoon into a lightly buttered and floured 9-inch square cake pan. Bake at 350° for 15 to 20 minutes or until the cake tests done. As soon as the cake is removed from the oven, brush the top with three additional tablespoons of port wine. Cool to room temperature. Make the glaze by mixing the listed ingredients. If desired, you can tint it a light color with a few drops of vegetable coloring. Spread evenly over the cake, sprinkle with additional chopped walnuts and let stand until firm. Cut pieces to desired size. *Yields about 16 squares.*

PORTUGUESE-STYLE MOLASSES COOKIES

3 cups flour

½ teaspoon salt

½ teaspoon cinnamon

¼ teaspoon allspice

¼ teaspoon nutmeg

1 tablespoon ginger

½ cup butter or margarine

1 egg

½ cup sugar

1 cup molasses

2 teaspoons white vinegar

2 teaspoons baking soda

½ cup boiling water

Mix the flour, salt and spices and set aside. Cream the butter or margarine with the sugar in a large bowl. Add the egg and beat. Then add the molasses, vinegar and the flour and spice mixture. Dissolve the baking soda in the boiling water and add this. If necessary, add enough additional flour to make a soft dough. Drop by generous spoonfuls onto a greased cookie sheet and bake at 350° for 8 to 10 minutes. These cookies are plump and soft when done.

Yields about 5 dozen cookies.

CHOCOLATE CAKE

1 egg

1 cup sugar

2 squares bitter chocolate

2 tablespoons vegetable shortening

1 cup sour milk (sour by adding a teaspoon vinegar)

1 teaspoon vanilla

1 teaspoon baking soda

1 cup sugar

1½ cups flour, sifted

1 teaspoon salt

1 teaspoon cream of tartar

¼ teaspoon almond extract

Beat the egg and the sugar together. Melt the chocolate with the shortening. Cool this slightly and add to the egg and sugar mixture. Thoroughly blend in the remaining ingredients, leaving the sour milk to be added gradually at the last. Pour the batter into a greased 9 x 12 cake pan and bake at 350° for 35 minutes. The cake may be served plain, cut into squares and sprinkled with powdered sugar, or frosted.

ALMOND BÔLOS

3 cups ground blanched   1½ teaspoons almond
   almonds   flavoring
3 slices of ground, dry bread   1½ cups sugar
4 eggs

You can blanch shelled almonds by dropping them into water which has just boiled. Remove them with a slotted spoon after a few minutes and slip off the skins. Pat the nuts dry, spread them on a cookie sheet and place in a 200° oven for several minutes. Grind them in a blender and measure out three cups of nut meats.

If the bread is not dry, it can be toasted and put through the blender or ground into crumbs with a rolling pin.

Mix the almonds and the bread. Separate the whites and yolks of three of the eggs and put aside the fourth. Beat the egg whites slightly and add to the almond and bread mixture, then add the almond extract and the sugar. Mix together until thoroughly blended. Take a full tablespoon of this mixture at a time and shape it into a ball. Make an indentation in the top of each ball with your finger. Now, beat the extra egg with the egg yolks and put some of this mixture into each indentation. Top with a blanched almond and bake at 350° for about 15 minutes or until slightly browned.

Yields about 4 dozen bôlos.

The Wines
of Portugal

Portugal has long been a great wine-producing country. In fact, the experts give Portugal credit for having discovered the importance of firmly corking the bottles and laying them on their sides for proper maturation.

Portuguese rosé wines have become popular in the United States during the past few years. They are light, not too tart, and like all rosés, may be served with either meat, fish or fowl without raising any eyebrows among wine perfectionists.

Rosés come in both still and sparkling versions and should always

be served nicely chilled. The very best rosés are labeled "reserva" or "garrafeira." It is a good idea to try the various brands available to decide which you like best.

If Portuguese rosé is not available, by all means substitute French or American rosé. As a choice to go with Portuguese food, you can't go wrong.

Another group of Portugal's table wines which are popular are the *vinhos verdes,* "green wines." Surprisingly, the wine is generally red in color, sometimes white and rosé, too. The "green" appellation signifies that these wines are young. They are usually bottled in the spring and are not meant to be stored too long. In fact, they are best when very young, in contradiction to most other wines. Since they are bottled while they are still fermenting, *vinhos verdes* are mildly sparkling, but not too bubbly.

Port is a fortified wine, one to which alcohol has been added. The port we encounter in the United States is "wood port." It has been aged in wooden casks rather than in bottles. We are offered two varieties — tawny and ruby. Properly, tawny port should have been aged in wood for twelve years, ruby port for seven.

Port is an excellent after-dinner wine and no better accompaniment can be found for Portuguese cakes and cookies on festive occasions.

Another famous Portuguese dessert wine is, of course, madeira, the product of that delightful island some five hundred miles off the Portuguese coast from which the wine gets its name. The lighter madeiras are good as aperitifs; the heavier, more familiar madeiras are served with desserts or as companions to a demitasse, when they should be sipped and savored.

I can think of nothing more pleasant than sitting beside an open fire on a chilly evening, sipping a glass of madeira and munching *trutas* or delicate *suspiros*, having earlier finished a cup of Portuguese soup and *vinho d'alhos,* accompanied by fresh, crusty Portuguese bread.

Index

Vorse, Mary Heaton, 37

Walnut Squares, 105

Wareham, Mass., 21
Wedding Cakes, 100
Wine, 14, 31, 79, 85, 111-113